WHY GAY GUYS ARE A GIRL'S BEST FRIEND

BY

Karen Rauch

AND

Jeff Fessler

A Fireside Book

Published by Simon & Schuster

NEW YORK LONDON TORONTO SYDNEY TOKYO SINGAPORE

FIRESIDE
Rockefeller Center
1230 Avenue of the Americas
New York, NY 10020

FIRESIDE and colophon are registered trademarks
of Simon & Schuster Inc.

Designed by Stanley S. Drate/Folio Graphics
Company, Inc.

Manufactured in the United States of America

10   9   8   7   6   5   4   3   2   1

Library of Congress Cataloging-in-Publication Data

Rauch, Karen.
    Why gay guys are a girl's best friend / Karen Rauch
  & Jeff Fessler.
        p.   cm.
    "A Fireside book."
    1. Gay men—Humor, Pictorial.   2. Friendship—
  Humor, Pictorial.
  I. Fessler, Jeff.   II. Title.
  PN6727.F47W58   1995
  741.5'973—dc20
            95-2045
            CIP

ISBN 0-684-80053-5

ACKNOWLEDGMENTS

Special thanks to Donna Allen for convincing us that our ideas were valid. Thank you to Jodee Stevens, Robb Anderson, and Ed Middleworth for giving us our big break. Thanks to our energetic and resourceful editor, Betsy Radin, at Simon & Schuster, for understanding what we stand for, and for her undying efforts to make our book a reality. Thanks to our brilliant agent/attorney Alton Burkhalter for getting us through the legal maze.

A special thanks to our families for instilling in us true family values and teaching us to be nonjudgmental, tolerant, and loving.

To Steve and Jamey

FOREWORD

For about a million years we've talked about doing something more creative than our normal everyday jobs as landscape architects. Designing greeting cards was one of those ideas. A quick trip to the card show in New York in the spring of '93 resulted in a successful relationship with Cardthartic, a Chicago-based greeting card company that specialized in the gay and lesbian market. One year later we had our own unique greeting card line at the New York show. Some of the cards we created were for parents to send to their gay children, and straight girls to send to their gay guy friends. Because of this unique subject matter we were covered on CNN and in numerous national magazines. A perceptive editor noticed a Cardthartic article in *Details* magazine, and suggested a book based on the cards. One year later, this book is the result of that idea.

We believe that relationships are special regardless of sexual orientation, age, race, and gender. Through our cards and our book we are proud to explore these relationships in the positive way they deserve to be portrayed.

A gay guy sends flowers just because you are you.

A straight guy sends flowers when he has screwed up big-time.

A gay guy's eye pattern when meeting a woman: looks first at the hair, then the earrings, then shoes, then makeup application.

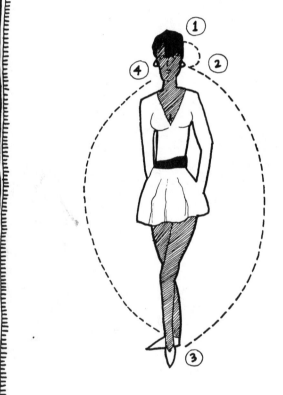

A straight man's pattern when meeting a woman: first looks at the right breast, then at the left breast, then one more glance at each.

A gay guy hugs you to show he cares.

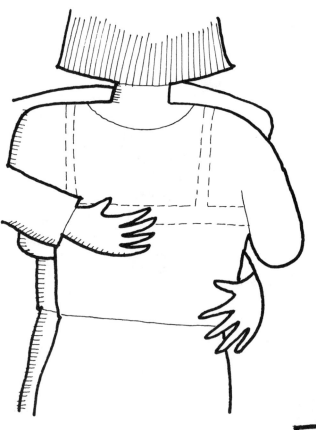

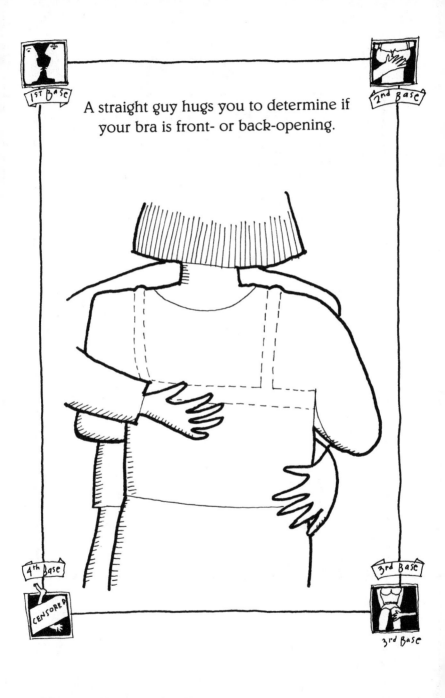

A straight guy hugs you to determine if your bra is front- or back-opening.

Gay guys will happily spend hours
helping you primp for that perfect look.

Gay guys leave the bathroom only after scrutinizing themselves in the mirror for any needed touch-ups.

Straight guys will walk around for hours completely unaware of the giant pee spot adorning their crotch.

You will want to brace yourself for the strange debris clinging to the Zest in a straight guy's john.

A number of straight guys have mistakenly used a lint brush to style their hair, and a few think mousse is what you hunt in a Canadian forest.

Gay guys understand the necessity of allocating 70 percent of all bathroom shelf space to hair-care products.

Gay guys aren't surprised when your long
list of desirable qualities in a mate
matches theirs.

A straight guy's list:

I WANT CHRISTIE BRINKLEY

Gay guys are warm and affectionate.

Gay guys share your idea that romantic weekends always include a moonlit walk.

A straight guy's idea of a romantic weekend always involves at least one stadium event.

A gay guy's reaction when you have PMS? Plenty of sympathy and an endless supply of Ben & Jerry's.

WAVY GRAVY • CHERRY GARCIA • RAINFOREST CRUNCH • AZTEC COFFEE • APPLE PIE • SWISS ALMOND CHOCOLATE •

CHUNKY MONKEY

55 Gallons

AU REVOIR • CIAO • GOODBYE • SEE YA! LATER • FAREWELL • ADIEU • IT'S BEEN REAL! ADIOS!

A straight guy's reaction to your PMS:
Call me when you snap out of it.

Many a straight guy's fondest childhood memory is knocking his pal's block off in Rock 'em Sock 'em Robots.

A gay guy will remember secretly wishing he could land on the cutest boy as he watched his sisters play Mystery Date.

A gay guy always remembers the first
ballet he attended.

A straight guy never forgets being chosen
for the lap dance at a bachelor party.

Mention "theater" to a gay guy and he immediately thinks of doing a quick weekend in New York or London.

Mention "theater" to a straight guy and he thinks of the Metroplex 27, where he's seen *Die Hard* eight times.

Gay guys like van Gogh and Van Cliburn.

Straight guys prefer Van Halen and Van Damme.

A straight guy will ask you to leave him alone while he watches his complete video collection of the Three Stooges—colorized.

Some straight guys believe that by show tunes you mean the theme song from *Bonanza*.

Many gay guys can sing any song, of any part, from any Broadway show ever produced. In costume.

Many straight guys think *My Own Private Idaho* is a documentary about the burgeoning Tater Tot industry.

Gay guys can always be counted on to see the most obscure artsy-fartsy films with you, particularly if there is a hunky male lead.

A gay guy can give you a play-by-play on who won what, who was wearing what, and why they shouldn't have.

Gay guys love Bette Davis eyes.

Straight guys love Suzanne
Somers' thighs.

courtesy of
twinkies

courtesy of
thighmaster

Gay guys regularly join you at the gym to keep your bodies trim and fit.

Gay guys can create at least ten variations of risotto.

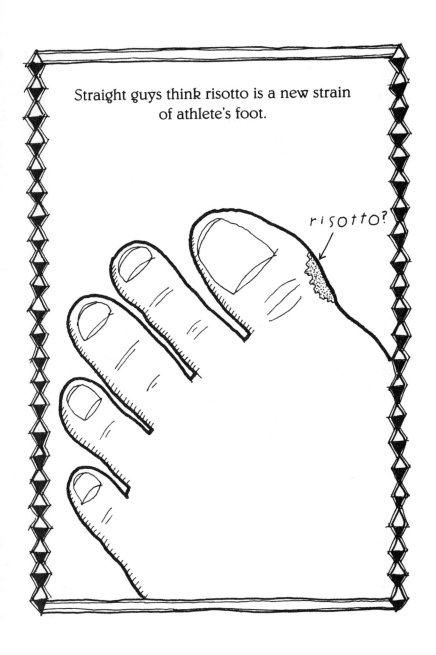

Straight guys think risotto is a new strain
of athlete's foot.

risotto?

Tiramisù filling: 1⅓ c. espresso (room temperature), ½ c. sugar, ¼ c. brandy, 2 egg yolks, 1 lb mascarpone cheese, 1 8-oz pkg. Lady fingers, 4-oz. Semi-sweet chocolate (shaved) ICING: 1 c. fresh whipping cream, 4 tsp. vanilla, 2 tbl. conf. sugar. Stir espresso, sugar & brandy in bowl until dissolved. (continued)*

Many straight guys assume tiramisù is some faggy new Japanese restaurant they wouldn't be caught dead in.

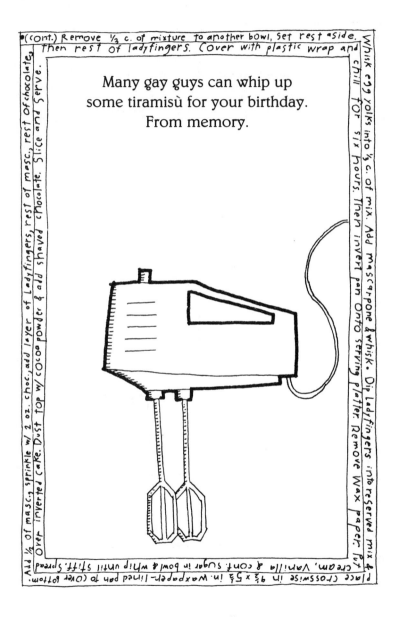

Many gay guys can whip up
some tiramisù for your birthday.
From memory.

(cont.) Remove ⅓ c. of mixture to another bowl, set rest aside. then rest of ladyfingers. Cover with plastic wrap and

Whisk egg yolks into ⅓ c. of mix. Add mascarpone & whisk. Dip ladyfingers into reserved mix & chill for six hours. Then invert pan onto serving platter. Remove wax paper. Put

place crosswise in 9¾ x 5½ in. waxpaper-lined pan to cover bottom. cream, Vanilla & cont. sugar in bowl & whip until stiff. Spread Add ½ of masc. sprinkle w/ 2 oz. choc., add layer of ladyfingers, rest of masc., rest of chocolate, over inverted cake. Dust top w/ cocoa powder & add shaved chocolate. Slice and serve.

Many gay guys grow purple globe basil, Italian parsley, chervil, and lemon balm to have handy for Tuscan cooking.

Many straight guys have purchased Chia Pets to impress women.

CH-CH-CH-CHIA!

Gay guys will spend hours preparing for the perfect dinner party, then talk for hours about who didn't show.

In the morning, gay guys offer you a steaming cup of espresso in a hand-painted demitasse.

In the morning, straight guys will mix
you up a little Nescafé if they can find
a clean spoon.

Straight guys think Iman is the name
of the clerk who sells them Ho Hos
at the 7-Eleven.

To hear gay guys tell it, your sense of style could put Iman to shame.

A gay guy's world comes to a screeching halt when Oprah's on.

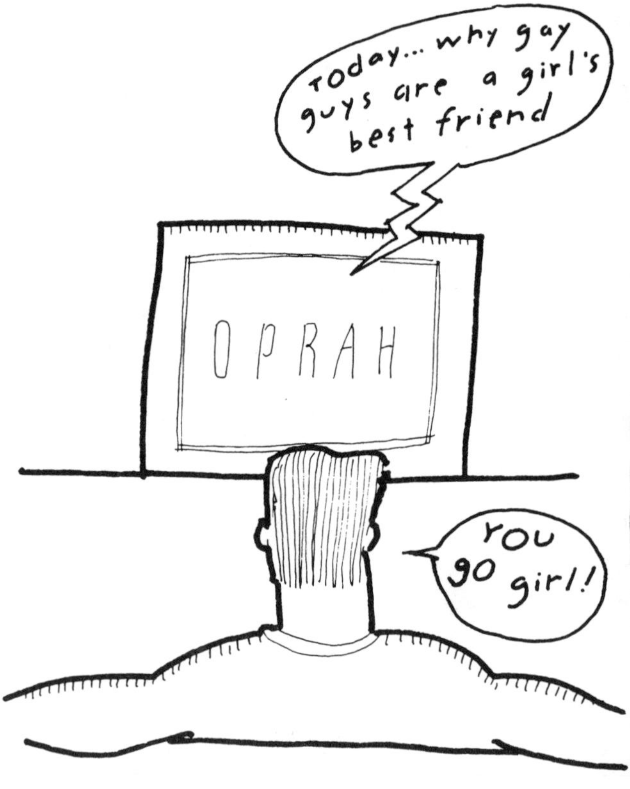

Straight guys will be late to their
own wedding if their alma mater is
in a bowl game.

Many a straight man thinks the world's problems can be solved by nuking the bastards.

Gay guys will say the world would be
a far better place if everyone were
given a makeover.

MODIFIED FLATTOP →

BRONZER →

DOUBLE Pierced Ear

Pride Necklace

Tattoo

TANK TOP

TONED MUSCLES

LIVE FAST DIE YOUNG

JERRY FALWELL (AFTER)

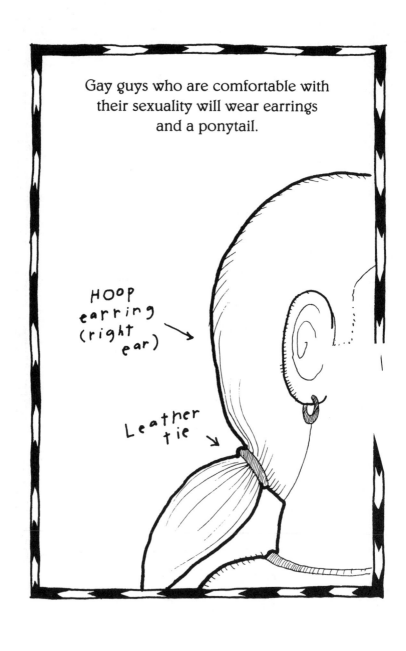

Straight guys who are very, very, very, very comfortable with their sexuality may consider wearing earrings and a ponytail.

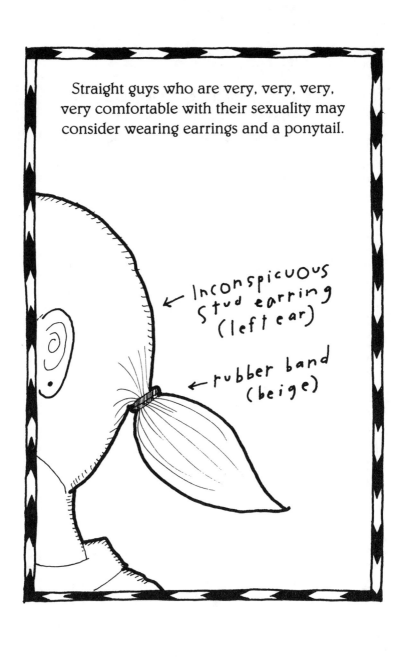

Gay guys know the obvious differences between chestnut, sable, taupe, sandstone, bark, and cocoa.

Straight guys will describe the same colors as brown, brown, brown, brown, brown, and brown.

Gay guys will hand-wash or send out
many of their fine clothes.

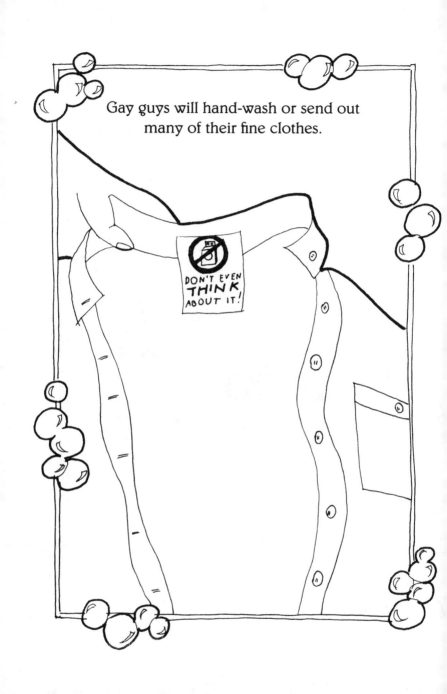

Straight guys usually divide their laundry into two categories: (1) the first load and (2) everything that doesn't fit in the first load.

Straight guys determine the day's ensemble by sniffing the armpits of various shrts balled up on the floor.

Gay guys will share their innermost secrets with you.

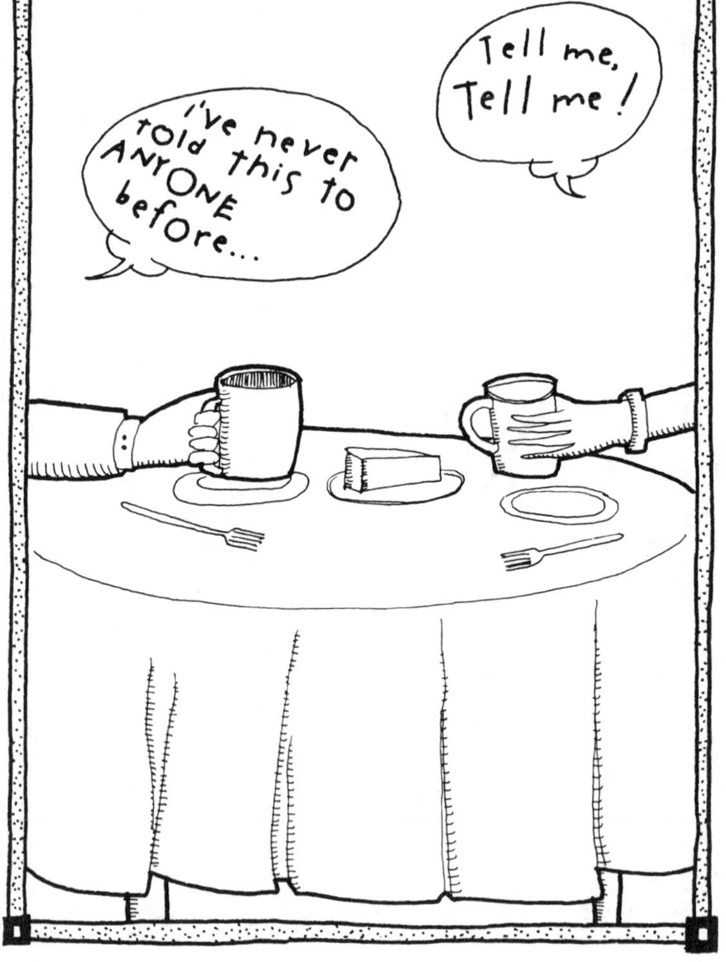

Straight guys will reveal their feelings of closeness by showing you the scar they got cleaning fish.

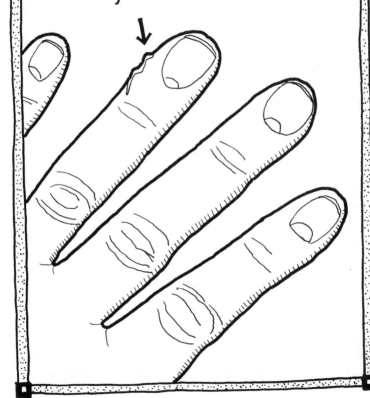

Scar (from largemouth bass)

Gay guys will send mushy cards to let you know how important you are to them.

A gay guy's idea of a thoughtful birthday gift for you is a watercolor of your cat.

A straight guy's idea of a thoughtful gift
for you is a pair of crotchless panties.

Straight sons have been known to forget their mom's birthday and try to make amends by picking up a mum with a balloon-on-a-stick at the Quik-Mart.

Eighty-one percent of gay sons can create
drop-dead birthday bouquets for their
mom in hues that complement her eyes
and the living room.

A gay guy's favorite plant? Obviously, the anthurium.

A straight guy's favorite plant? The venus flytrap—it sucks the guts out of bugs.

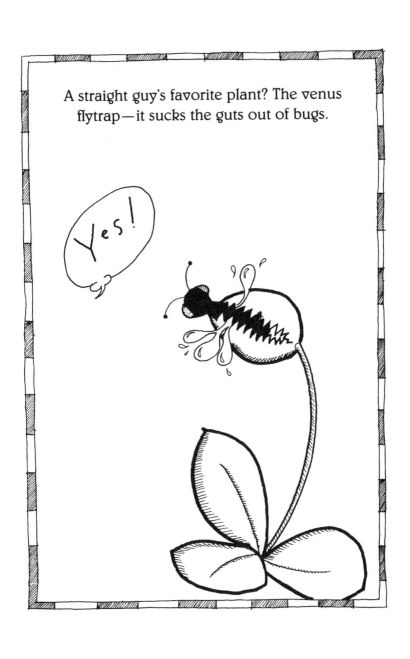

Check a gay guy's mailbox and you'll find *Architectural Digest, Condé Nast Traveler, The Smithsonian,* and *Martha Stewart Living.*

Check a straight guy's mailbox and you'll find a *TV Guide* and the latest Ace Hardware sales flier.

Straight guys like wilderness weekends because they get to ignore all forms of personal hygiene.

ALL-PURPOSE CAMPING TOILETRY KIT

TOILET PAPER

MOUTHWASH

DEODORANT

A gay guy's idea of roughing it is going to the Hilton without reservations.

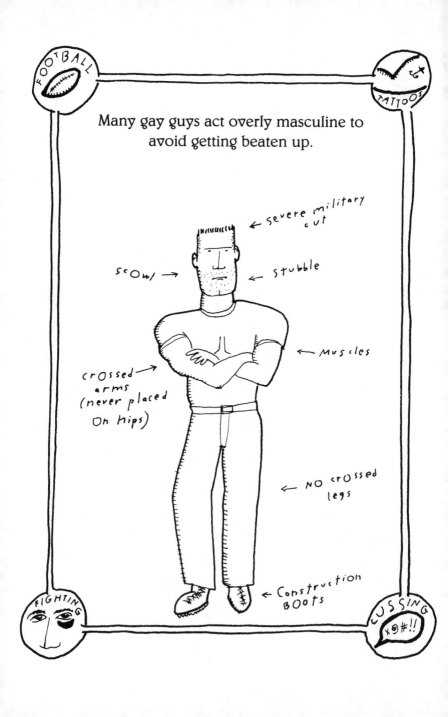

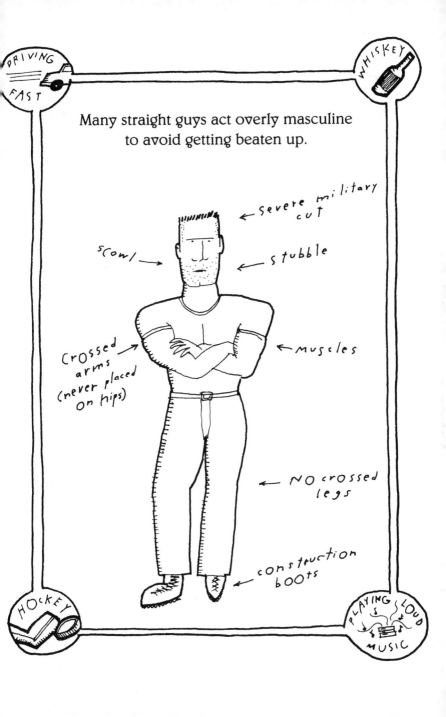

Straight guys will pull off the road to watch heavy machinery.

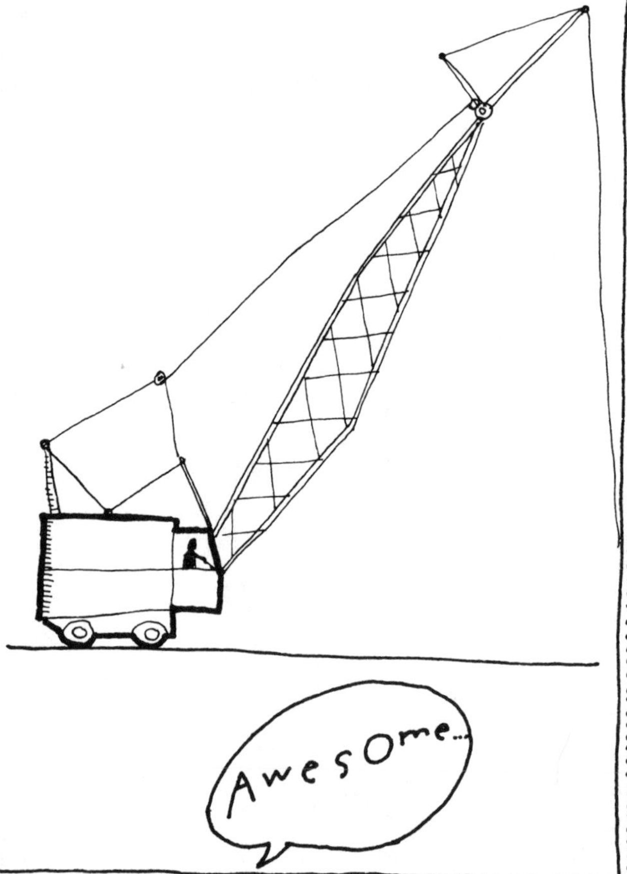

A gay guy will travel back roads with you to discover out-of-the-way cafés and craft fairs.

A straight guy takes you interstate nonstop unless he feels the need for a pecan log or another gross of bottle rockets.

Gay guys have usually participated in a demonstration for civil rights.

Straight guys have most probably started a food fight.

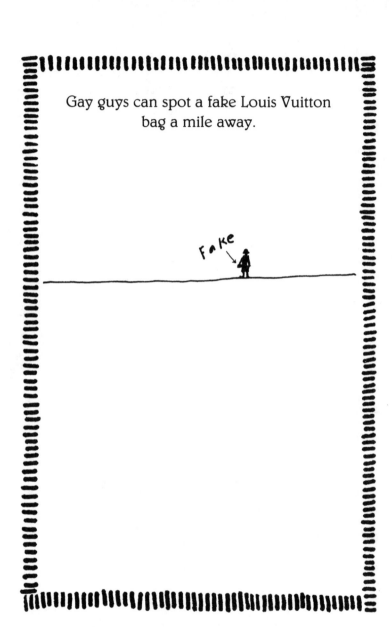

Straight guys can spot Air Jordan knockoffs two basketball courts away.

Gay guys always offer a shoulder to cry on and a helping hand when you need one.

Straight guys may suggest you go shoot some hoops. . . . Well, it works for them.